Ecstatic in the Poison

Ecstatic in the Poison

NEW POEMS

Andrew Hudgins

SEWANEE WRITERS' SERIES / THE OVERLOOK PRESS

First published in the United States in 2003 by
The Overlook Press, Peter Mayer Publishers, Inc.
Woodstock & New York

WOODSTOCK:
One Overlook Drive
Woodstock, NY 12498
www.overlookpress.com
[for individual orders, bulk and special sales, contact our Woodstock office]

NEW YORK:
141 Wooster Street
New York, NY 10012

∞ The paper used in this book meets requirements for paper
permanence as described in the ANSI Z39.48-1992 standard.

Library of Congress Cataloging-in-Publication Data

Hudgins, Andrew.
Ecstatic in the Poison : new poems / Andrew Hudgins.—1st ed.
p. cm. — (Sewanee writers' series)
I. Title. II. Series
PS3558.U288E23 2003   811'.54—dc21   2003050681

Book design and type formatting by Bernard Schleifer
Printed in the United States of America
FIRST EDITION
ISBN 1-58567-429-X
3 5 7 9 8 6 4 2

For Wyatt Prunty

If ever the search for a tranquil belief should end,
The future might stop emerging out of the past,
Out of what is full of us; yet the search
And the future emerging out of us seem to be one.
                                        —WALLACE STEVENS

Question: If you could live forever, would you? And why?

Answer: I would not live forever, because we should not live forever, because if we were supposed to live forever, then we would live forever, but we cannot live forever, which is why I would not live forever.
     —MISS ALABAMA, at the 1994 Miss Universe pageant

CONTENTS

III

IN

In

When we first heard from blocks away
the fog truck's blustery roar,
we dropped our toys, leapt from our meals,
and scrambled out the door

into an evening briefly fuzzy.
We yearned to be transformed—
translated past confining flesh
to disembodied spirit. We swarmed

in thick smoke, taking human form
before we blurred again,
turned vague and then invisible,
in temporary heaven.

Freed of bodies by the fog,
we laughed, we sang, we shouted.
We were our voices, nothing else.
Voice was all we wanted.

The white clouds tumbled down our streets
pursued by spellbound children
who chased the most distorting clouds,
ecstatic in the poison.

I

The Snake

When we open,
the snake opens
with us—old
rumble gullet,
acid tunnel.
We are the snake's
garden—his garden,
his gate, his adam
and eve—and he,
the snake, plays
the role of the snake.
We are his tree
of the knowledge of
good and evil,
which is desire,
which is good and evil—
desire, which
is appetite,
which is the snake
that feeds then starves us,
and, thus, we are
his paradise,
which is emptiness,
lumen, the light
we fill with darkness,
the labyrinth
of reptile running
entrance to exit—

rumble gullet,
acid tunnel,
the great dissolver,
the snake god
hungering
in the blood garden.

The Lake Sings to the Sleepless Child

Come walk
          where no one walks. Come dance
across the lilies while quick fish nudge
the bottoms of your feet.
                    Come quickly.
You're light,
          my darling—buoyant, nothing—
and in my hands I've held a rowboat,
a rowboat holding
                    mother, father, you—
all in my hands, light
                    as the mist
that rises from me in the blue moonlight,
and wafts
          through dark pines to your window
whispering,
          Come, daughter, come
and soar into the world beneath your feet,
where swift
          fish slide between your fingers.
You too will swoop like the swallow here,
or dart and
          hover like the dragonfly.
You love your blue and yellow light
but deeper down, the green
                    light gleams
above you like an emerald sun,
and deeper yet
          the plush black glow

reveals all living things are one,
and you'll be that one thing, my lovely,
as you fly deeper,

                       deeper down,
swooping and soaring slowly

                              on the current's
unfurling breeze. Come, lean your light
foot

     on the lily, and rise forever
on the dark unhurried waters of descending.

Beneath the Apple

The house a-tilt with laughter, jazz,
and tipsy friends, I eased
into the yard, and took a breath
of dark, chill evening, pleased

to leave behind smoke, drink, and noise.
I lumbered to the apple
in the darkest corner, near the fence,
and underfoot a windfall,

crushed to paste, infused the air,
its sweetness lush with rot.
(I ought to take it down, the apple.
But that's an afterthought.)

Too much to drink and my house full,
I leaned against the tree
and stared back into yellow windows,
perplexed—why now?—to see

old friends, whose lives I know too well
and who know mine. We share
long histories but decreasing time.
We make good laughter bear

what laughter can, which is a lot.
I saw my smiling wife
finger a neighbor's bright new hair
and risk an honest laugh.

A hundred feet away in darkness—
and I knew what she'd said
and what her laughing friend said back,
her hair a fevered red.

I leaned into the teeming tree,
fumbled, and emptied myself
onto its peeling bark. The dog
strolled over, took a sniff

and emptied himself too—two mammals
depositing their salts
against the boundary tree. I named
and then unnamed my faults

as I stood under unplucked fruit—
a spiteful woodland god,
I thought. Or tried to think. The god—
or was it I?—guffawed.

I sauntered up the lawn in joy,
a ghost. Nothing was mine.
The house, the friends, the night. I loved
that moment: Dead. Divine.

The Cadillac in the Attic

After the tenant moved out, died, disappeared—
the stories vary—the landlord
walked downstairs, bemused, and told his wife,
"There's a Cadillac in the attic,"

and there was. An old one, sure, and one
with sloppy paint, bald tires,
and orange rust chewing at the rocker panels,
but still and all, a Cadillac in the attic.

He'd battled transmission, chassis, engine block,
even the huge bench seats,
up the folding stairs, heaved them through the trapdoor,
and rebuilt a Cadillac in the attic.

Why'd he do it? we asked. But we know why.
For the reasons we would do it: for the looks
of astonishment he'd never see but could imagine.
For the joke. A Cadillac in the attic!

And for the meaning, though we aren't sure what it means.
And of course he did it for pleasure,
the pleasure on his lips of all those short vowels
and three hard clicks: the Cadillac in the attic.

Day Job and Night Job

After my night job, I sat in class
and ate, every thirteen minutes,
an orange peanut-butter cracker.
Bright grease adorned my notes.

At noon I rushed to my day job
and pushed a broom enough
to keep the boss calm if not happy.
In a hiding place, walled off

by bolts of calico and serge,
I read my masters and copied
Donne, Marlowe, Dickinson, and Frost,
scrawling the words I envied,

so my hand could move as theirs had moved
and learn outside of logic
how the masters wrote. But why? Words
would never heal the sick,

feed the hungry, clothe the naked,
blah, blah, blah.
Why couldn't I be practical,
Dad asked, and study law—

or take a single business class?
I stewed on what and why
till driving into work one day,
a burger on my thigh

and a sweating Coke between my knees,
I yelled, "Because I want to!"—
pained—thrilled!—as I looked down
from somewhere in the blue

and saw beneath my chastened gaze
another slack romantic
chasing his heart like an unleashed dog
chasing a pickup truck.

And then I spilled my Coke. In sugar
I sat and fought a smirk.
I could see my new life clear before me.
It looked the same. Like work.

The Ship Made for Burning

For ten days while he was in the ground
we women sewed rich garments for him.

                                               We men
drank night and day and made for him a ship
made for burning, and we asked his girl slaves,
"Who will die with him?"

                        and I said, "I,"

and we two attendants groomed her and washed her feet.

What did you do when your father left the earth?

And I who am the slave girl drank and sang,
and gave myself to leisure.

                           When the ship was made,
we removed the lord's corpse from the earth. We dressed him
in soft boots, a caftan studded with gold buttons,
and we propped him on a cushion in the ship
and surrounded him with meat, his blades, his dog.
We each lay with the slave girl and we each said,
"Tell your master I've done this for love of him."

What did you do when your mother left the earth?

I made that vow to each man as he left me.
They raised me over the doorframe and I said,

"Behold, I see my mother and my father,"
and they lowered me and raised me again and I said,
"I see my ancestors seated at the feast,"
and they lowered me and raised me again and I said,
"I see my master seated in Paradise,
and Paradise is beautiful and green.
He calls me. Take me to him."

What did you do when your brother left the earth?

They carried me into the pavilion with my master,
and, thick with sweet beer, I lay against his chest
as I had lain when he was yet alive,
though never for an entire night, never receiving
the whole of his great warmth, not being his wife,
but neither was I his body slave, she
who merely washed his gray hair, cooked his meat,
and scraped the day's sweat from him. I bore him children.

What will the living do when you pass on?

And we strangled her and stabbed her and burned the ship
made for burning, launched it on red waves,
and we drank as it burned down to cinder and ash,
beyond the reach of insects, and we raised a birch post
and wrote the name of the Rus king on it, and we departed.

Embroidering My Thesis

As I wrote and wrote and wrote, I saw
it wasn't even wrong.
The reason *Othello* terrified me
was missing. All year long,

at ten, I mixed two stiff drinks, watched
the news with my ex-wife,
and stitched tea towels: smug cucumbers,
cross-eyed tomatoes, a knife,

and, beside a crock of marmalade,
a nervous orange. A large
peel spiraled off the orange and curled
against the crock. The orange,

like me, was scared. As I stitched and brooded,
half-listening to the news,
Othello rebuilt, against my thesis,
its horrifying virtues:

delineations of delight—
if it is, in fact, delight.
Increments of intricate
instruction. Is that right—

I'd learned something? I couldn't find
true ways of praising it.
Language failed me. I failed language—
distrustful, but not silent.

On Christmas eve my brother asked,
Are you still reading shit
that didn't happen? No, well, yes—
but I'd outwitted it,

I'd hoped, by thinking only words
had left me terrified.
That night I asked my wife a question
and felt her answer guide

a knife through my mistaken work.
The orange feared the knife
that carved it into usefulness.
I've learned to love my wife.

The Children

She reared back, pitched the empty fifth
against the wall. Why not?
The poems had all been cursed and spanked—
or taken out and shot.

We shied back from the spraying glass.
Except there wasn't any.
The bottle bounced off drywall. We laughed
because it wasn't funny,

which made it funny. Very funny.
We joked about the low
romantic gesture. She grabbed the bottle,
placed it on a pillow,

conveyed it to the sidewalk, lay it
gently on hot concrete,
and smashed it with a rock. We stomped
the glass beneath our feet.

We danced atop the jagged shards.
We sang, and then sang louder.
We tangoed, flamenco'd, cha-cha-cha'd
the glass to bursts of powder.

Next week we each brought in a shy
young poem, its pink face slapped,
its hair slicked back, its blubbering
half soothed. It sang. We clapped—

applauded dutifully and long,
encouraged it, admired
its spirit. Then down to business: knives,
whiskey, gunshots fired.

Southern Literature

She hunched in the backseat and fired
one Lucky off the one before.
She talked about her good friend Bill.
No one wrote like Bill anymore.

When the silence grew uncomfortable,
she'd count out my six rumpled ones
and ask, noblesse oblige, "How ah
your literary lucubrations

progressing?" "Not good," I'd snarl. My poems
were going nowhere, like me—raw,
twenty-eight, and having, she said,
a worm's eye view of life. And awe—

I had no sense of awe. But once
I lied, "Terrific! *The Atlantic*
accepted five." She smiled benignly,
composed and gaily fatalistic,

as I hammered to Winn-Dixie, revving
the slant six till it bucked and sputtered.
She smoothed her blue unwrinkled dress.
"Bill won the Nobel Prize," she purred.

If I laid rubber to the interstate,
and started speeding, how long, I wondered,
how long would she scream before she prayed?
Would she sing before I murdered her?

Would we make Memphis or New Orleans?
The world was gorgeous now, and bigger.
I reached for the gun I didn't own.
I chambered awe. I pulled the trigger.

The Chinaberry Trees

. . . and oh, the chinaberry trees in niggertown!
—E. Welty to K. A. Porter, 1941

Under the flowering chinaberry,
we parked, and drifted on the tide
of hot scent ebbing toward a dream
we shied from. Mystified,

we gave ourselves to fragrance, eyes shut
to barrel fires and wicks
flickering in smoky shacks.
What was there to fix

our eyes on—purple flowers hidden
in the leaves and the leaves in darkness?
We didn't have to understand
what we had witnessed. Fragrance

numbed and suspended us among
then-the-past and then-
the-future, and then, which was the now
we levitated in.

I've never been so far transported,
as I was there, under trees
I wouldn't have on my green lawn.
By May, the fetid berries

rot in the hot shade underneath
the lowest branches. Crows
riot in the reeking poison,
not harmful to them of course—

shrieking like Furies in the fruit,
mating and making mess.
Azalea, redbud, cherry grace
our lawns. And our success

drove us, March nights, past barbecue
and juke joints. We parked outside
tilted shotgun shacks, eyes closed,
and breathed deep, nullified,

releasing ourselves to perfume, knowledge
out of context, abstraction
our talking couldn't dim. We lived
in the pilfered Indian

gift of the chinaberry—the tree
uprooted from my lawn
but thriving there in niggertown,
lush and left alone.

When a gray battered truck scraped past,
we awakened, blinking. Once,
thrilling us, a pistol shot rang out,
and after, in the silence,

a raw harmonica exploded,
someone's ridicule
sucked backward through the instrument,
the laughter lurid, cruel,

and magnified to frightening music—
except we weren't afraid
or chastened. We reveled in its rage,
and hung on its harsh fading.

Arcadia

> BURGLARY: *A book of classical mythology of unknown value was reported stolen from a carport storage room in the 3400 block of Arcadia Drive between 11 a.m. Saturday and 4 p.m. Sunday.*
>
> —The Tuscaloosa News, August 22, 1996

While rooting in the storage room
for frozen peas, canned peaches,
I scanned the shelf where *Classical
Mythology* once slumbered.
It was gone. I'd labored over it:
Zeus underlined and Hera lit
with yellow ink, while I pursued
the panicked wood nymphs, then fled with them
in terror, a panicked nymph myself
until I turned into a swallow,
a reed, a nightingale,
and I escaped, escaped not just
the lust-mad god I thrilled to be
but escaped the library and the life
I was preparing for,
and which I've lived. But even here,
even in Arcadia—
peaceful and heavily policed
Arcadia—he'd come for me,
the deity of sleep and dreams.
I'd studied him in school and passed
that test, as I had passed
all other tests. The god of thieves,
the escort to the underworld,

the messenger. Why had he come
to rouse me from my life,
a life where in the morning
I knew I would be granted evening,
and in the evening I knew
I would be granted morning—
this knowledge an altar
on which I'd sacrificed
an animal: my life
up to that moment? Suddenly
I saw the drowsy thief reclining
beneath the red oak in my yard,
as if, because he is a god,
he owned my oak, owned it because
his feet are shod with wings. "Thief! Thief!"
I yelled. I was crying,
then I had fallen at his feet,
and his ludicrous small wings
ruffled at my breath. He laughed
and fanned the pages of the book.
"Remember when you were a swan,
a reed, a nightingale? Remember?"
He held the empty book before me,
the pages drained of every terror
I'd given and received—
"I've come with a message: *Run!*"
I started running and I changed
to a cat, a greyhound, and a fox
before, as a deer, I leapt the fence,
flew, a crow, to the blackest woods,
slipped through the sharpest bramble—mink—
racing before the sly god, changing
with every step to something terrified.

The White Horse

Unswerving, neither graceful
nor ungraceful, running at
the absolute last limit
of its power, a white horse
pounds across the desert
and without pausing plunges
down a cliff, its hind legs pumping
left, right, blasting clouds
of dust, its legs and chest
dyed red with dust. It's tearing
straight through me like a spear.
Why am I not screaming?
No. It hammers past,
red hooves churning wild grass,
which flies, and with the red dust
settles on my hair, my shoulders.

Stop. I'm sorry. I was afraid.
Restart the vision.
                              Horse
rockets down torn red cliff
and I step in front of it.
It hits me, kills me. No,
absorbs me, and we are running
across the red desert,
running at the absolute
new limit of our power,
gaining speed, our white
face shadowed like a skull,

our cheeks hollowed with pure
velocity. Join us.
Make us faster, faster,
O faster . . .

II

Grandma's Toenails

Don't gawk! *Why not?* It's wrong.
But still I peeked. Beneath her red
distended ankles, glossy
with ruptured veins, and isolated

at the ends of feet so thick
they burst from her black shoes, I saw,
in rude and furtive glimpses,
Grandma's toenails. I loved each flaw

she hated. Nails humped and buckled
on calluses, and I was wild
to stare at them. Thick, yellow
with dirty light—what a world

they almost opened! A world
of crippling labor. I was berserk
to stare without restraint
on flesh she had deformed with work.

Thus rage. Thus meat for supper.
Thus love. Beneath their surfaces—
quartz, topaz, almost amber—
I could darkly sense old weaknesses

purged from her armored body,
and one sharp beating could not control
my urge to violate
my bloodline's bartered blood-clenched soul.

Come to Harm

We were driving from one state to another,
my father already there,
and we'd been singing hymns, hymns
soaring from the car

with our joy at passing on to glory,
where loss would turn to gain,
our wounds would heal—and in the silence
after our last refrain

my mother said she'd known, known
before the call had come,
her father had died. She'd felt his passing.
She'd known "he'd come to harm"—

as if Death had enticed him. As if
he had returned to drinking
and wed Death's hootchie-cootchie girl,
Death's crude seducer. Thinking

"True Tales of the Supernatural!" I wondered
how I could tell this story
and make friends shudder. Or failing that—
I was this predatory—

how I could make them laugh. I flipped
"There's a world beyond this world"
to "My mother is a silly woman"—
and back again, as we hurled

through darkness singing songs of hope.
She told her sacred story.
We sang. We laughed. She died. I wept.
Her story isn't mine. I'm sorry—

and not—about how I have told it.
Who knows what's coming after?
There may be another world. There may.
There will be laughter.

The Weight of the Rain

Eight floors below, a woman strides by,
her blond hair streaked with blood.
She's talking to herself and nodding.
Sirens pass. Clouds scud

across the morning, black with rain,
which ticks against the window.
The crows' sharp laughter outside fills
the inside. Like fevered skin,

the window blazes when there's sun.
Now rain beads there instead,
and I am cold. Crows, sirens, drizzle.
Hand clamped to her blond head.

Her wound a deep attentive ear,
her hand a telephone.
My books and the TV's cold blue screen
ignore rain, crows—they've flown—

and thunder. I had forgotten thunder.
This morning I heard its groan
and couldn't place it. Her wound an ear,
her hand a telephone.

By the time I reach the street, she's gone,
though I am here, a savior.
What is she saying to the wound?
What is it telling her?

The cupped ear hears its own thin hearing,
an airy hollow tone—
her ear and mine a single wound,
our hands a telephone.

Or so it seems to me this moment
as I stand in the rain,
staring violently both ways
for the woman and her pain.

Coins and Ashes

We need two hundred bucks! Mom yelled
and swept the table clear
of coins I'd stacked in dollar piles.
Flesh burning in the air.

We what? Dad screamed. *Two hundred bucks?*
The coins rolled toward the shadows.
Dad kicked them. Mother punched his face.
They shared slow looping blows,

until, exhausted, they collapsed
against each other's shoulder,
teetering, as I watched the coins
glow and begin to smolder,

splashed bright across linoleum—
star clusters that foretold
what I'd be doing every day.
Blazing uncontrolled,

blue fire, like twin blowtorches, split
my parents' spines. Hard flame
enveloped them, and under it
they swayed, dancing. They became

one tall blue flame that scorched the ceiling.
The lights exploded. Curved
pearlescent flakes of glass rained down
on me as I, unnerved,

watched flames that had begotten me
shrink, gutter, and then die
to a pile of ashes at my feet.
I found each scattered dime

and quarter. I found and ate them all.
And since I was their son,
I choked down the ashes. I gagged and wept
but I ate every one.

The God of Frenzies

The tall boy shook and shimmied across lunch tables,
shouting at us to shout.
"Jeez, what a jerk," I thought, but I still shouted.
I couldn't stop myself.
Strapped to his torso, pinned up and down his legs,
blue pompoms snapped and sizzled. We screamed with him,
and as we roared, he rode
our screaming, swam in it like water, soared.
We shook our pompoms at the living pompom,
and—mad, ecstatic—he
burst into flame. The boy inside the flames
froze one half-second as he changed
from flesh to fire. He raced
across the tables and leapt toward us. I thought
it was stagecraft, part of his act.
Who would have thought that what looked true was true?
I couldn't hear his screams above our screaming.
I couldn't see him flopping on the floor.
Later we heard a story:
a match flipped at the swirling paper. A joke.
Though I know now that I was seeing terror—
a boy burning on a table—
I remember joy, the boy flung gratefully
to his full blazing length onto the air
as if he thought the air would hold him.
At that false remembered moment,
I saw terror and ecstasy,
and I would ask the god of frenzies why,
with both choices before him, he chose terror,
though I know there was no reason. He simply chose.

Two Strangers Enter Sodom

Those who'd seen them told the others,
and we gathered at Lot's doorsills
to watch them eat. They had just dipped
their fingers into lentils

and their slender fingers glistened with grease.
Lot bathed their feet, small feet
just barely dulled with earth, releasing
light trapped beneath a sheet

of fine dust. Slowly he released them,
each small foot oiled and dried.
"I want them," someone whispered. Another,
like an ardent echo, sighed.

Another said it openly.
"We want them! Send them out!"
we shouted. We'd seen unearthly beauty
enter a house, bathe, eat,

prepare to sleep. Some might stop at looking,
but others, seeing it,
would reach out and, touching, they would take it,
even if taking it

destroyed what they desired. We surged
against the strangers, screaming,
and the angels calmly struck us blind
with the light of our own dreaming.

Still reaching out, we touched each other:
coarse cloth, coarse hair, coarse skin—
and cringed from it. We pawed cool air
for the lost celestial men,

whose footfalls faded lighter, lighter
till they were light's own light
departing—or so it seemed to us
in our god-dazzled night.

Bucephalus

What solace daughters are! They die—
yes, they die in fever
mewing softly as feeble kittens,
or die in childbirth over

a long night, bucking like wild horses
Death's breaking to the halter.
Or for no reason they take to weeping
in private. They whimper, falter,

drift away. But they die here,
at home among their kind.
But sons, who knows where they lie buried,
deposited behind

great Alexander like hot turds
dropped from his horse, his horse
whose name is a household word, our sons
a stench in Persian gorse.

We loved our daughters' fearless laughter.
We love their ashes. We love
their graves, which we can stand beside,
weep over, plant an olive.

Behemoth and Leviathan

"Can you draw out Leviathan
with a fishhook?" Yahweh sneers.
We have drawn out Leviathan.
At first with terror, then cheers,

and then the grunted curse of work.
We've hunted him to nothing.
We've drawn him with a fishhook, Lord,
and then we've stilled his thrashing.

We've locked Behemoth in a pen
for children—and his horn
we've ground for an aphrodisiac.
We've plucked it like a thorn.

Earth-shakers wallow in zoo mud
and every morning amble
to their steel troughs and wait for food,
hungry but hugely gentle,

and the great ship-destroyer sits,
a jar of yellow oil
in a bright museum in Salem, where
I saw myself recoil,

and gag at ancient rancid fat.
We've drawn his mighty tooth
and etched it with the memories
of his efficient death.

Deep is shallow, distant close,
the predator defended,
the fierce incomprehensible
now fiercely comprehended.

But in their looming disappearance
they're what they've always been:
Behemoth and Leviathan,
and chaos at the margin.

Beatitudes

Blessed is the Eritrean child,
flies rooting at his eyes for moisture. Blessed
the remote control with which I flipped on past.
Blessed the flies whose thirst is satisfied.
Blessed the parents, too weak to brush away
the vibrant flies.
     Blessed the camera crew
and blessed the gravity of Dan Rather, whose voice
grows stranger with every death he sees. Blessed
my silence and my wife's as we chewed our hot
three-cheese lasagna.
     Blessed the comedies
we watched that night, the bed we slept in, the work
we rose to and completed before we sat
once more to supper before the television,
a day during which the one child died
and many like him. Blessed is the small check
we wrote and mailed. Blessed is our horror.

Silver

You and your mother polish it
and put it up. Using silver
would be purse proud, hoity-toity,
but it's a comfort to her

to know it's there and capable
of glowing in elegant candlelight,
though candles are only there for show.
Some nights, when the house is quiet,

you open the lid and study it:
place settings pressed and canopied
in navy velvet. They look like knives,
forks, spoons, but filigreed

and ornamented beyond use.
Thus art. Thus beauty. Therefore concealed,
the word itself used carefully.
On a day not yet revealed,

Grandma will say, "Get you some silver
out of the drawer, honey." She'll wince,
regard your elegant young wife,
and say, "It don't make sense.

It's flatware. We just call it silver."
That's why you clean the brightness, boy,
doing a job that you back then
and I, not to be coy,

don't understand. Interpret it,
and you'll forget your mother's hands
blue with polish. You'll forget
the heavy blue-tipped strands

of hair stuck to your face, which make
your mother laugh, and you'll forget
your own blue-smudged, foreshortened face,
the face that your eyes met

appraisingly in brilliant spoons.
Understand, and you'll destroy
memory with meaning, even
your undreamed memory

of Mother's blue lips and the bed
she withered in, which you haven't seen,
as I have. Understanding is
obliteration. Morphine.

A drug to use if you should need it.
Your mother pressed in navy velvet.
Thus art. Thus beauty. Therefore concealed,
and held against our forfeit.

In the Cool of the Evening

Among lilies I am Jehovah,
the Lord God walking in the cool of the evening,
delighting in every green that grows, sorrowing
for those that fail. I am Christ the healer:
I spray for black spot and white fly, pluck aphids,
and when the leaves turn crisp I pluck them too
and drop them in the dirt to soften and return.
The Lord God walking in the cool of the evening.

With books I am merely the student,
saying why, why, why—exasperating myself
and even the long-dead with my questions.
But among dianthus, I am the decider:
Not here, but there. Not you, but something else.
The Lord God walking in the cool of the evening.

Beside bellflower, poppy, phlox, I keep the deathwatch.
Among lilies I am the slow mourner for the soft bulb
rotting in damp clay, the quiet griever
over fire blight in the pyracantha—fire blight,
canker, scale—and when I fail as Christ, I succeed
as the adversary, root-digger, extirpator—
the Lord God walking in the cool of the evening.

Beyond branch tips, where they scrape the sky,
I see the sheets are white, starched, and my skin is yellow,
yellow and going gray. Down the row,
the Lord God walks in the cool of the evening,
delighting, sorrowing, healing, failing to heal.
I am very calm, I am almost not afraid.
I look neither toward him nor away from him,
the Lord God walking in the cool of the evening.

The Aiming Mark

A pigeon-colored dawn, and two generals march—
are marched—
                    between sandbags to a wooden post.
Klimovsky notices
the post is splintered. Soon they'll need a new one.
His hands are lashed behind him,
                                        his shoulder boards
hacked off with a bayonet.
An aiming mark is pinned above his heart.

Let us deploy, they'd begged. *Let us*
                                prepare.
Our German neighbors are our allies now,
Stalin answered.
                    We can't insult our allies.

In six days,
            three hundred thousand Russians died
as the Wehrmacht plunged through spring,
                                unslowed, toward Moscow.
Gray sky turns rose. Klimovsky
                            stains his pants
and General Pavlov snaps his bloody head
from side to side, trying
                    to fling his blindfold.
Twelve soldiers lock their bolts.
The captain promises them all two weeks of hell
if one, just
            one shot hits below the waist.

They're boys. He

knows them. Boys.

They'd do it out of curiosity.

In six weeks they'll be corpses. And the captain.

The commissar awakens in his tent,

stretches, yawns,

and jots down a good phrase.

He mulls it over, then erases it.

It must

be perfect for his valiant men.

It must be poetry.

The Fourth Year of an Eight-Year Drought

Let us consider the Carthaginians.

Let us consider the Carthaginians
entering the fourth year of an eight-year drought.

Blown sand scours the granary's inside walls.
Sand
      rattles in the empty oil pots, and rakes
the dying groves. Sand frolics in the well.

Let us consider the Carthaginians
as they examined their lives and sacrificed.

Swaying to the rhythmic
               clash of tambourines,
drums, trumpets, they march the length of their dry city.

Let us imagine we're Carthaginians.
Let us imagine we march through our dry city.

To drown the wailing we would never wail,
bell-ribbons
             snap above our heads. We kiss
and tickle, tease and pet our fretful infants
so they'll be laughing, legs
                  kicking with delight
when the priest pulls the knife across their throats.

Let us imagine willing sacrifice.

We offer them to the god like lambs or bulls,
which have not
                        pleased the god. Our tiny souls
unfold when, singing, we lay our first-born sons
in the god's bronze arms.
                                    No one sobs or moans.
No one taints the sacrifice. No one
begrudges
            the first lamb, first
                            dove, first
                                    peach, first
full bushel of summer grain—the dearest offering
inadequate
            for rain, wheat and the sons,
whose elders, sacred warriors, saved our city.

Let us understand we live in Carthage.
Let us understand our sacrifices.
It is the fourth year of an eight-year drought.

Under the Influence of a Minor Demon

Power was allowed to demons
for a limited time. Their house
is made of fire, their souls are water,
and you can hear them hiss.

As a boy I leapt the bonfire's flames,
and the flames, in pleasure, leapt
to greet me. I'd thought that we were friends.
I curled in their ashes and slept.

I told myself that we were friends,
not soldiers. For thirty years
bits of Hitler's skull
reposed—lost souvenirs—

in a matchbox marked "Blue Ink for Pens."
Sekander carried home
in a vat of honey. Napoleon shipped
in a barrel of port. Is flame

a man or demon? Our nightmares alter
the historical report.
In wind, cold ashes leap cold embers.
Their time has not seemed short.

Cattails

A stand of cattails: brown heads
                              erupting seed,
silk tufts unfolding
                    from coarse velvet. I stopped
and studied them while all my friends walked on
except
          for one who lingered, agitated,
and watched me watching, palms locked on her elbows,
her body bent.
                    "You can't write about them,"
she said. "I saw them first."
                              But who am I
to tell this story, when I remember saying
"I don't want to read about this later"
to another poet,
                    half our buttons
                                        half
unbuttoned? She called my name. And who was I
when later in that walk
                    I leapt in a grave,
a fresh one waiting for its corpse, the name
known,
          though not to us, the stone
                                        unchosen?
"Jump in! It's just
                    a hole in the ground," I said
as everyone drew back and no one laughed.
The one who lingered at the cattails
                                        has yet
to write about the cattails. In her poems

I'm Death, beckoning from the grave.

                            I did.

But I crawled out again. I'm Lazarus.
And since nobody offered me a hand,
I'm Christ. I died

               and raised myself. And no,
she wasn't wrong. I'm also Death.

                       And Adam.

The names now never stop, nor the naming.

Land of the White Crows

"The people there are much like us,"
he said. "In war they're brave," he said.
"Like you." And he broke off a crust
and speared a slab of yellow fat.
"But the people over there," he said,
"sleep on the ground. For ornament
a man there wears an iron collar,
and tethered to it by a chain
a crow sits on his head. The crows,"
he said, "the crows are solid white.
White crows!" In our puzzled hush he grabbed
the goat's foreleg and pulled it free.
He chewed as we debated white crows.
One white crow is a marvel, easy
to comprehend. But a flock of crows
the color of a flock of swans
disturbs the words we use for words.
Do white crows still eat carrion?
And how, if crows are white, could we
sing the old songs, describe the night?
He filled a horn with our good cider.
Could coal be white? Could snow be hot?
Since he passed through two springs ago,
we cannot stop debating crows
or the hungry stranger at our fire
who, with white crows, transformed our world
to air, then wind, as he passed through
from somewhere strange to somewhere strange.

A Flag of Honeysuckle

From the brush pile I wrestled brittle limbs
and shoved
            them in the chipper. As I worked down
the six-month heap, a thin
               green flag sprang up—
a slip of honeysuckle. I tugged
           it; it
resisted,
        white threads infiltrating dark earth—
and suddenly I was on the Burlington
Street bridge in Iowa, watching
              a cottonwood.
Spring floods had flushed it from the riverbank
and trundled it downriver till it snagged.
Its leaves,
        fed by the heavy river, drooped,
drooped in the June, July, and August heat,
but held their ashen green,
            and from the bridge
I conjured with the possibilities:
I am the tree. I am uprooted, adrift.
I made the world a tool
           for my crude use.
It's how I've lived when I have had to, slapping
one feeble, transitory understanding
before another—
        each meaning a restive step
from what I was to what I hoped to be—
remarried? out of debt?—arriving now

at now: remarried,

                paid, and contemplating

a ratty flag of green that waves its standard

above my brush.

               Rebirth? The weak

                           triumphant?

Blind nature? They rise

                 so easily to mind

without the force of need to make me fight them,

old friends

            returning from old understandings,

whipping this twig of honeysuckle into fragrance.

Mango

1

The slippery flesh slides underneath the knife.
    Slice off the sides,
and score them to the skin. Press. Tidy cubes
    of flesh pop up
and you may eat them gracefully. Or snatch it.
    Devour it.
Devour it as juice streams down your arms.
    Until it's broken,
the fruit is neither nourishment nor joy—
    broken on teeth,
and lavished on the smooth, adoring tongue.

2

"Who cares how someone makes the bed?" I sneered
about my girlfriend's
    poem, and I walked home,
where for four months I'd written and rewritten—
eleven
    to forty lines, then down to eight,
in free verse,
    blank,
    and rhymed tetrameter—
a poem on how to eat a mango.
    I'd never seen
a mango.
    It was a metaphor for art,
I said, how we consume the world's soft flesh.

Night after night the pale

                  poem waxed and waned

till I abandoned mangoes

                and quit popping

imagined cubes of fruit from tough green skin.

Last week I read her splendid poem again—

starched cotton,

              cool sheets to rumple and ignite

with meaning. It loves its subject and itself.

Goodbye

        to metaphor, I thought. Goodbye

to *like*. Goodbye

            to *blank* is *not blank*. Goodbye

to *Is* harrumphing through a foreign film.

But trope returns us

            to what it isn't—as kisses

return us

        to what our lips are pressed against.

Mango. Made bed. Kiss. All these

                closed doors

on which I knock until

           my knuckles crack—

while life exacts this late apology.

Asleep with the Dog

Curled into my side—
tight, part of me—she whimpers,
twitches, growls,
and in her unbroken dream,
and my broken one,
we bull through saw grass, blast
through burning bramble,
murderously fixed
on rabbit—not
the tossed ball and contemptible
stick of this afternoon
and the one before and the one after.
She shakes the dream-prey.
She prances with joy, joy
in the death-work,
trembles with it, blood-joy,
can't contain it, can*not*
contain it, awe, and I dream
I tremble her trembling,
my brain bright with her fire,
her desire mine
in my half-dream of imperfect
and knowable otherness—
and if I do not tremble
I can dream it
for a moment longer, I can linger
for a moment longer,
in this lie I have loved with my life.

Flamingos Have Arrived in Ashtabula

Flamingos have arrived in Ashtabula.
Or one has. Bending to fetch the morning paper,
the mayor saw it standing on her lawn,
poised one-legged like a plastic bird
jabbed in the grass, and thinking it a joke,
she laughed. It lumbered, lurched into the air
and sailed across her back fence, rising pink
against the near-pink Ashtabula dawn.

Flamingos have arrived in Ashtabula,
blown here we think by a line of thunderstorms—
a scrap of pink confetti on the wind—
except those storms were months ago. No zoo
reports a lost flamingo, and it doesn't seem lost.
It circles the airport tower, lands on the courthouse,
and stalks a drainage ditch behind the mall,
where people linger with binoculars
to watch a flamingo feed in Ashtabula.

A local bar, once Dewey's Hometown Lounge,
is now the Pink Flamingo—pink chairs, pink drinks.
Stuck in the ceiling, hundreds of plastic pink
flamingos hang over us upside down, observing,
while we sip pink gin and ponder the waitresses'
pink tee-shirts. From them even pinker pink
flamingos with sequin eyes return our gaze.
Flamingos have arrived in Ashtabula.

The tropical bodies resplendent against gray sky,
the languid beating of long wings—we see them
in our imagining and dreams, and now
in daylight we scan the sky, the bogs, the ditches
for a hint of pink or parrot-green, a red
that shimmers. Turquoise. Electric yellow eyes.
Or I do. I speak for no one but myself.
Flamingos have arrived in Ashtabula.

Sun through Sunflowers

The late sun drops beyond
sunflowers. Suffused light
ignites the yellow petals
with solar fire—gaudy
halos topping rough
green angels. They remind me
of something. Isn't this
how the moment always slides,
now slipping off in search
of then, or next? The flower
dead last winter—gone,
now returned and soon fading:
What is it? The rise and fall
of all that falls and rises?
Or is the dying light
transfixed on flowerheads
simply death? Death
because we watch them blaze
into October, coarser
and coarser, till packed with seeds
they droop, blacken, drop.
But death's not what I thought of
before I started thinking,
the flowers on fire with light
that shines, for all my purposes,
eternally. The sun-
flowers' yellow fills
with yellow light—rank
backlit ephemera
ablaze, aglow, aghast
against its august autumnal dying.

Wasps in August

With the death craze on them, wasps in August
rage near their paper nests,
defending them from raccoons, jays,
and other ravening guests

that hunger for the feast—and risk
the deathwatch wrath of wasps.
They'll swarm on anything to save
the spit-and-tissue wisps,

their soft spawn pulsing as they swell.
And in their common need
to gorge the hardening larvae in the nest,
they stand and bleakly feed

on broken apples in the yard.
They don't pause, don't buzz, don't
fly up in fear and light again.
They simply stand and eat,

then ferry nectar to the nest.
Death calls, and they're replying,
The nest, the nest, the nest, the nest.
The easy job is dying.

A Joke Walks into a Bar

A joke walks into a bar and takes a pun—
a ten-inch pun—out of his pocket. He orders
a beer. The pun kicks it into his lap.
Another beer. The pun dumps it. Amazed,
the barkeep laughs, then whispers to the joke:
"Hey, Mack, where'd you get him?"

                                   And suddenly
the joke was tired. He no longer cared to talk
about the witch, or how—young, dumb, and drunk—
he'd begged for a ten-inch prick. He sighed, paid,
and left the bar, the pun still racing up
and down the counter kicking over drinks.

The joke sold his whoopee cushions, rubber chicken,
even his Bozo shoes. And the next time
his left foot hit a black banana peel,
he didn't hang suspended in midair
but fell. A broken coccyx, fractured skull.
In pain he drank, groaned, drank, cursed, drank, and, drunk,
exposed himself to uncurious schoolgirls,
groped boys in public restrooms. Nothing helped:
somebody somewhere will laugh at anything—
a hair between your teeth, a sore that's shaped
like Florida, a child who screams exactly
like a scorched parrot when some drunk strokes his bottom.

The joke washed, shaved, joined six AA groups,
the Methodist Church, and the Rotary Club.
But he kept slipping back to desert islands.

Whorehouses. Church. For hours he sat on barstools
drinking Coke and questioning his friends.
He wanted to know what happened to the chicken
once it had crossed the road. Did it stay there?
Did it go back? Or was the chicken locked
into an endless cycle of road crossing
and recrossing because the side he'd left
was now the other side? The chicken didn't know,
and the joke felt cruel for asking. Old steps he'd danced
so elegantly now felt like old steps. He was,
he thought, like an aging playboy at a brothel.
He wanted the fat madam to sit near him
and tell him how much fun he used to be
when he was young and flush.
                    As he left the brothel,
the April wind whipped his hat from his head.
It tumbled down Main Street, and he remembered
how, all his life, he'd chased it, the hat his master,
everyone cheering the hat. He stood and watched,
till the wind gave up and swept his tempting hat
into the river. He turned and walked toward home,
and halfway home, alone, he started laughing.

After Workshop

we drifted to the Union, arguing:
A's divorce, B's suicide attempt,
M's sleeping with N, O, and, strangely, X—
how should we write our lives? Simplify
the action and complicate the motivation,
we learned in class. But young, or young enough,
we loved the obvious: fear, lust, and rage.
Complicate! Complicate!—
as if we were sole authors of our stories,
as if, in those first drafts, we understood them.

But soon we're sitting at our desks, uncertain
if we're remembering or making up.
What's simple? What's complex? And thus we move
from Hemingway to James's *Golden Bowl*—
too many motivations—much like my own
dwindling happy life, in which I write
less for the old rage, which I miss, and more
for the unreliable delights
of breathless Subject crooning his desire
to coquettish Object. Oh, her cold heart!
And how she teases him! I love them both,
as I love doing what my masters did,
the masters whom I used to fear and envy
because they were my masters.
How I fear and envy my new masters:
Monsieur le Sujet, Mademoiselle Objet—
his ardent songs and her elusive twitter.

The Poet Asserteth Nothing

The poet asserteth nothing. This elegy's
the best damn poem I've ever written. *The poet
asserteth nothing and therefore* it doesn't matter
my father isn't dead, or even ill.
*The poet asserteth nothing and therefore
never lieth*, Sir Philip Sidney wrote,
and drunk at parties I cornered nervous friends
and badgered them. Did they think *poets asserteth
nothing and therefore never lieth?* I knew
that I asserteth much and lieth plenty.
I think he'd like it if he ever saw it.
I knew that poets asserteth much and lieth
with everyone they could. I knew that truth's
a lie because it can't contain this world,
the next, the truths opposing it, raw grief,
my father's death. *The poet asserteth nothing
and therefore never lieth*—both assertion
and lie. True lie. And death will make it truer.

The Long Ship

Death's settled in my suburbs: weak ankles
just a little weaker and the fingers of my right hand just
a little more like unoiled hinges in the cold.
Death's moved into my right shoulder as a flame.
I tease it, taunt it, test it: Can I carry wood?
Can I still throw the ball? How far and for how long?
What's the new price? Higher, but not too high.

Death, darling,
                    you've been gentle up till now.
But after the first kiss I return, we know
how your seductions go: each tender kiss
a little coarser. Each night a little further:
caress to rough insistent stroke. Each qualm
and modest scruple brushed aside till metaphor
gives way to metamorphosis—from one
hard, lived cliché to one nobody lives:
Death's built his long ship, he's raised his black
sail over me, and what ship doesn't love
a steady wind, and what ship doesn't love the white
wake curled behind it like lilies on a black stem?

Piss Christ

Andres Serrano, 1987

If we did not know it was cow's blood and urine,
if we did not know Serrano had for weeks
hoarded his urine in a plastic vat,
if we did not know the cross was gimcrack plastic,
we v ould assume it was too beautiful.
We would assume it was the resurrection,
glory, Christ transformed to light by light,
because the blood and urine burn like a halo,
and light, as always, light makes it beautiful.

We are born between the urine and the feces,
Augustine says, and so was Christ, if there was a Christ,
skidding into this world as we do
on a tide of blood and urine. Blood, feces, urine—
the fallen world is made of what we make.
He peed, ejaculated, shat, wept, bled—
bled under Pontius Pilate, and I assume
the mutilated god, the criminal,
humiliated god, voided himself
on the cross, and blood and urine smeared his legs—
the Piss Christ thrown in glowing blood, the whole
and irreducible point of his descent:
God plunged in human waste, and radiant.

Blur

Storms of perfume lift from honeysuckle,
lilac, clover—and drift across the threshold,
outside reclaiming inside as its home.
Warm days whirl in a bright unnumberable blur,
a cup—a grail brimmed with delirium
and humbling boredom both. I was a boy,
I thought I'd always be a boy, pell-mell,
mean, and gaily murderous one moment
as I decapitated daises with a stick,
then overcome with summer's opium,
numb-slumberous. I thought I'd always be a boy,
each day its own millennium, each
one thousand years of daylight ending in
the night watch, summer's pervigilium,
which I could never keep because by sunset
I was an old man. I was Methuselah,
the oldest man in the holy book. I drowsed.
I nodded, slept—and without my watching, the world,
whose permanence I doubted, returned again,
bluebell and blue jay, speedwell and cardinal
still there when the light swept back,
and so was I, which I had also doubted.
I understood with horror then with joy,
dubious and luminous joy: it simply spins.
It doesn't need my feet to make it turn.
It doesn't even need my eyes to watch it,
and I, though a latecomer to its surface, I'd
be leaving early. It was my duty to stay awake
and sing if I could keep my mind on singing,

not extinction, as blurred green summer, lifted
to its apex, succumbed to gravity and fell
to autumn, Ilium, and ashes. In joy
we are our own uncomprehending mourners,
and more than joy I longed for understanding
and more than understanding I longed for joy.

The Hawk above the House

The hawk hung low above the house,
appraising:
           prey or not
                 prey? Not.
Then it swung up, veered eastward—gone.
That moment
           I too ached to open
my great imagined wings and arc
against the sun's arc, reversing it
and following its bright track back
through dawns and darkness
                       till I soared
in sunlight above the stucco box
I sat on as a boy,
          and there
I'd fold those gold imagined wings,
plummet, and from
              my father's roof
I'd watch the boy who watched for me.

O, he'd have given anything
to fly: the hawk
          exploding on
the sparrow or the sparrow,
               frantic,
threading through the black-green cedars.
He'd have given anything to fly,
the rapt boy
          staring at the air,
imagining if he could imagine

hawk thought,
>   deciding no, then knowing
it was impossible, a pure
extension of himself to wings
and cold predation,
>   he tried—and failed,
but not
>   completely, as he had thought,
and here I am to tell him so.

Out

My father cinched the rope,
a noose around my waist,
and lowered me into
the darkness. I could taste

my fear. It tasted first
of dark, then earth, then rot.
I swung and struck my head
and at that moment got

another then: then blood,
which spiked my mouth with iron.
Hand over hand my father
dropped me from then to then:

then water. Then wet fur,
which I hugged to my chest.
I shouted. Daddy hauled
the wet rope. I gagged, and pressed

my neighbor's missing dog
against me. I held its death
and rose up to my father.
Then light. Then hands. Then breath.

Acknowledgments

The American Poetry Review: "Behemoth and Leviathan."

The American Scholar: "Asleep with the Dog."

The Atlantic Monthly: "The Hawk above the House."

Boulevard: "Sun through Sunflowers."

Crazyhorse: "A Joke Walks into a Bar."

Descant: "Flamingos Have Arrived in Ashtabula," "The Weight of the Rain," "Under the Influence of a Minor Demon."

DoubleTake: "The Long Ship."

The Georgia Review: "Two Strangers Enter Sodom."

The Hudson Review: "Bucephalus," "The Fourth Year of an Eight-Year Drought," "The Ship Made for Burning."

Image: "Blur," "In the Cool of the Evening."

The Iowa Review: "Beneath the Apple."

The Kenyon Review: "The Aiming Mark," "The Lake Sings to the Sleepless Child," "A Flag of Honeysuckle."

The New England Review: "The God of Frenzies," "Silver."

The Paris Review: "Beatitudes," "The Cadillac in the Attic," "The Snake."

The Sewanee Theological Review: "Land of the White Crows."

Slate: "Come to Harm," "Piss Christ," "Wasps in August."

Southern Cultures: "The Chinaberry Trees."

The Southern Review: "Cattails," "Coins and Ashes," "Grandma's Toenails," "In," "Southern Literature."

TriQuarterly: "After Workshop," "Mango," "The Poet Asserteth Nothing."

The Writing Path: Poetry and Prose from Writers' Conferences, edited by Michael Pettit (Iowa City: University of Iowa Press, 1995): "Embroidering My Thesis," "The White Horse."

"Blur" was reprinted in *The Best Spiritual Writing 2000*.

I am grateful to the many friends who read these poems and offered useful comments on them—and I count my wife, Erin McGraw, as one of those discerning friends. I want to thank Bob Jones for his meticulous copyediting, which saved me from many embarassments, and I want to offer a special thank you to Ellen Bryant Voigt, who read the book twice with a shrewd and discriminating eye.